None the Wiser

A Comedy for Women

Anthony Booth

A SAMUEL FRENCH ACTING EDITION

SAMUEL FRENCH

FOUNDED 1830

SAMUELFRENCH-LONDON.CO.UK
SAMUELFRENCH.COM

FOR AMATEUR PRODUCTION ENQUIRIES

UNITED KINGDOM AND WORLD
EXCLUDING NORTH AMERICA
plays@SamuelFrench-London.co.uk
020 7255 4302/01

Each title is subject to availability from Samuel French,

depending upon country of performance.

CHARACTERS

SISTERS: JEAN VISITING SISTERS: ANGELA
         EDITH   ROSE
         SUSAN
         BESS
         VERA

Place: The living room of Stonegate Convent, containing: a fire-
            place, pouffe, settee, small table for flowers, etc., a long
            table on which is a telephone, two plain wooden chairs.
            There is a door leading to the rest of the house and another
            leading to the front door. A window overlooks the front
            door and drive.

Scene 1:   Late Afternoon

Scene 2:   The same, two weeks later

NONE THE WISER

Scene 1

As the curtain rises, JEAN is sitting on the pouffe below the fire reading a
paper. EDITH is mending some clothing seated on the settee. BESS is asleep
alongside her. There is a long silence.

EDITH   Anything interesting in the paper?

JEAN   No, the world seems to be full of trouble.

EDITH   It always has been.

JEAN   I'm sure we never had the number of murders we have, these
                days.

EDITH   I expect we did only they weren't found out.

JEAN   Yes, there could be something in that.

EDITH   Any more news of the raid on the Securicor office?

JEAN   No, the police say they have a lead but that means
                nothing of course. It says they got away with a hundred
                and fifty thousand pounds.

EDITH   As much as that?

JEAN   So it says.

EDITH   There's no honesty these days.

JEAN   I agree.

                  (They lapse into silence. BESS suddenly snores. They look at her then carry on. After a moment she snores again even harder.)

JEAN   Oh no, I just couldn't do with an afternoon of her snoring. Nudge her.

                  (EDITH nudges her. She stirs, half asleep.)

BESS   (murmuring)   What – er what?

                  (EDITH nudges her again even harder.)

                  (waking up)   Eh?

EDITH   You were snoring.

BESS   (crossly)   I was not.

EDITH   You don't know, you were asleep.

BESS   Well I'm entitled to a little nap if I want to.

JEAN   Nobody said you weren't. You were snoring that's all.

BESS   (muttering)   No privacy that's the trouble.
                  (She turns over and falls asleep again. After a moment she starts snoring again.)

                  (EDITH and JEAN raise their eyes resignedly. SUSAN enters left, she has a large bowl of flowers which she puts on the table and starts to straighten them out.)

JEAN   Oh what lovely flowers, where did you get them?

SUSAN   A dear old lady in the market gave them to me.

EDITH   How nice of her.

SUSAN   Yes wasn't it. She put them into my arms and said, –
                  'May they bring you a lot of happiness my dear'. You
                  know, it quite restored my faith in human nature.
                  (She stands back a little.)   There, how do they look?

EDITH   Very nice, just what we wanted for that table. Makes the
                 place look very homely.

SUSAN   I've just made the tea, I'll bring it in.   (She goes out.)

                 (JEAN goes to the window and gazes out.)

JEAN   You know, we could grow our own flowers here   it's a huge
                 garden.

EDITH   We won't be here long enough.

JEAN   No., I suppose not. How long are we staying?

EDITH   I don't know, a few weeks I suppose.

JEAN   You know there is no reason why we should move really,
                 providing we organise things properly. After all we
                 couldn't find a better spot, right off the beaten track yet
                 close to town. It has so many advantages. I love
                 gardening and I'd like to get this place into shape. What
                 do you think?

EDITH   Well, if you want my honest opinion, I find gardening
                 deadly dull.

BESS   (suddenly)   Me too.

EDITH   I thought you were asleep.

BESS   Which only goes to show how wrong you can be.

                 (SUSAN enters with the tea on a tray which she puts on the
                 table.)

SUSAN   Here you are. Who's going to be mother?

JEAN   There is a joke there if only I could think of It.

SUSAN   Yes and in bad taste probably. All right, I'll do it.

                 (As SUSAN pours VERA enters left. VERA is their leader
                 and at the moment is obviously annoyed.)

VERA   (angrily)   All right, all right, come on, own up -
                 who's been thieving my gin?

EDITH   Are you accusing us?

VERA   What does it sound like? You can't keep anything these
                 days. Nothing's private.

SUSAN   Well it's not me, vodka's my tipple, you know that.

VERA   What about you others?

JEAN   We've only just got in.

VERA   Well somebody's nicked it - about four good tots.

          (BESS gives a muffled hiccup. VERA glares at her
          suspiciously then moves to her.)

          How long have you been back?

BESS   Er - er - about two hours.

VERA   (triumphantly)   I thought so. Let's smell your breath.

          (BESS sighs and puffs slightly towards VERA who staggers
          back under the wave of gin.)

          Cor blimey, you smell like a ruddy distillery.

BESS   Sorry Vera, but you weren't here and my tongue was
          hanging out for a wet. I'll replace it, I'll get you a full
          bottle tomorrow.

VERA   (ungraciously)   There's no need to do that - sorry I
          blew my top but nothing irritates me more than petty
          pilfering.

          (SUSAN laughs.)

          What's so funny?

SUSAN   You. We are all pilferers. Why this sudden holier than
          thou attitude?

VERA   (firmly)   You don't understand. Nicking things from
          shops is our livelihood, nicking amongst ourselves is
          dishonest and deceitful.

EDITH   Well that's splitting hairs if you like.

JEAN   No, I disagree, I think Vera's right. We've got to trust
          each other. That is the strength of our association.

VERA   Exactly. Well, what luck with today's run? Got your
          lists?

ALL   Yes.

VERA   Let's have them.

(They pass them to her and she sits at the table glancing through them and murmuring her appreciation at times.)

Not bad, not bad at all. Solly should be pleased with this lot. Hullo, I seem to be one short. Where is yours Bess?

BESS   I er – haven't checked my bag yet, it's still in my room.

VERA   Well get it.

BESS   (sighing)   All right. Here, hold my tea will you? (She hands her cup to JEAN and moves to the door.) Won't be a moment.   (She hiccups, is about to apologise but finds VERA glaring at her. She gives a sort of shrug of resignation and goes out.)

EDITH   She'll have to go.

VERA   I must say I'm a bit worried about her.

JEAN   Oh she's all right.

VERA   I'm not so sure. Don't forget, one mistake can fix us all and she's not the most reliable of people.

SUSAN   Especially if she gets on the Red Biddy.

VERA   She hasn't been drinking that again has she?

SUSAN   I don't think so.

VERA   I hope not, that's fatal. You can smell it for miles.

JEAN   You can say that again.

VERA   At a pinch you can say that whisky or brandy had to be taken medicinally, but you can't explain a nun reeking of methylated spirits. That's stretching credibility too far.

SUSAN   Personally I think she's a menace. Couldn't you put her out to grass, Vera?

VERA   I've thought of that but it's too risky. She's liable to get stinking in a pub somewhere and blurt out the whole issue. Can't you see the headlines in The News of the World? 'Gang of expert shoplifters disguised as nuns, unmasked'. I should think they'd put that one on page four. No, whatever the risk, it's safer to keep her with us. The devil you know.

SUSAN	I suppose you are right.
VERA	All the same, I think you've got a point. In future we had better not let her work alone. Someone must always go with her.
EDITH	I agree. She always makes a mess of things anyway. Look at that turn up last month when we tried that jewelry job at Harrods.
JEAN	What was that?
EDITH	Oh I forgot, you weren't with us then. Well, Vera worked out a master plan. On paper it just couldn't miss. Harrods had a wonderful diamond display in their jewelry department and at a definite time I was to be in the electric control room and pull the master switch, blacking out every light in the store. During this Bess was to switch a case of rings from the counter with a duplicate case of paste ones she had in her bag. She had fifteen seconds to do it in, too.
JEAN	I suppose she forgot the fake rings.
EDITH	No, worse than that – oh when I think of it, I could weep.
JEAN	Well, what happened?
VERA	Edith got into the control room without any trouble but was challenged by the electrician, so she said she's lost her way and was looking for the loo. As the bloke was directing her, she came over faint as it were and collapsed against the switch board and sort of pulled the master switch to the off position plunging the whole place into darkness. The old boy was so upset about her collapsing that he forgot to switch on for nearly half a minute.
JEAN	So she had all the time in the world. How did she muff it?
VERA	You'll never believe this, she never even got to the jewelry department.
JEAN	Couldn't she find it?
VERA	Oh she knew where it was because we had a dummy run to time everything the week before.
JEAN	Well what then?

VERA   (closing her eyes at the memory)   She stopped in the
                television department and got so intrigued watching a
                demonstration of colour T.V. that she forgot all about the
                time.

                (JEAN laughs heartily.)

                Yes, we can see the funny side of it now but that little lot
                cost us five hundred quid. Solly had already placed the
                stuff a fortnight before we did the job.

                (BESS enters right with a large black oilskin shopping bag.)

                Let's have it here.

                (BESS puts it on the table.)

                Sue, make the list as I call it out, will you?

SUSAN   Okay.   (She takes out a small pad and pen.)

                (VERA takes the articles out of the bag one by one.)

VERA   One gent's wrist watch - one pair of Zeiss binoculars.
                (To BESS.)   Not bad.

BESS   I thought you would be pleased with those.

VERA   (picking again)   One - no, two Japanese transistors -
                Solly likes those, they always sell. One large bottle of
                Lentheric - one luxan hide handbag - one plastic handbag -
                (Holds it out in distaste.)   - what do you want to bring
                rubbish like that for?

BESS   I thought it was genuine crocodile skin.

VERA   (contemptuously)   Plastic, forty-two and sixpence -
                one silver bracelet - one gold bracelet - one packet of
                aspirin?

BESS   (quickly)   I bought those.

VERA   Whatever for?

BESS   To distract the girl while I whipped the shavers.

VERA   Oh.   (She pulls out two electric shavers.)   Two
                electric shavers - what's this?   (She holds up a small
                packet.)   Birth pills?

BESS   What!

VERA   Have a look.

BESS   I don't know where those came from.

                (VERA shakes her head in despair. She puts her hand in
                the bag again.)

VERA   One Black and Decker drill.

BESS   That's the lot.

VERA   Not too bad, I suppose, for a morning's work. The
                binoculars are the only things that will bring real money.
                However, it all adds up.   (She hands the bag back to
                BESS.)

BESS   Ta.

JEAN   Your tea is cold I'm afraid.

BESS   Never mind, I'll brew myself a fresh pot in a minute.

                (VERA studies the lists again.)

VERA   Well, I'd better ring Solly I suppose.

                (VERA dials the number and waits. While she is waiting
                BESS hiccups again. VERA sighs but says nothing. After
                a moment a voice answers.)

                Can I speak to Mr Cohen please? -   Very well, I'll hold -
                Solly? - Vera. Are you alone? -   good. How did you
                do with the last lot? -   Look cut out the spiel - what
                lolly have we got coming to us? -   (Astounded.)
                How much!   - well you thieving git -

                (The voice obviously becomes agitated at the other end,
                she holds the receiver away from her.)

EDITH   He sounds hopping mad.

VERA   He is.

SUSAN   What's he saying?

                (VERA listens for a moment then imitates SOLLY.)

VERA   'Sharp businessman I may be, but robber, never.'

                (They all smile. VERA listens again.)

                All right, Solly, calm down - that's better. Now how

much? A hundred and seventy quid! That stuff was worth over seven hundred - I'll tell you what, we'll take three hundred - two seventy then - no, no - all right two fifty, it's a deal. When can we have the lolly? - Well I can collect it tomorrow - where? Lyons Corner House, Edgware Road, eleven o'clock - oh and Solly, none of your fivers this time, I want it all in used oncers - Yes, and you'll be the death of me too. 'Bye.   (She puts the phone down.)   Crafty so and so, anyway we got him up a bit. So the share out this week works out.at fifty quid a head.

JEAN	That's not at all bad. Mark you, we've earned it.
VERA	I'll give you that. If it isn't a rude question, what do you do with yours?
JEAN	Put it in the post office.
VERA	That's a bit dodgy isn't it? They are liable to suspect big amounts each week.
JEAN	Oh not really, I've got seven books in different names.
VERA	Oh that's all right then.

(The phone rings again, VERA picks up the receiver.)

(sweetly)   Mother Superior, Stonegate Convent - (Changes tone swiftly.)   Oh, it's you again - what? - You must be joking.   (She puts the phone down.)

SUSAN	Who was that?
VERA	Solly again.
BESS	What did he want?
VERA	He says he's had an order for a Mark Ten Jag.
SUSAN	Oh, I'd like to do that. Now that really is a challenge.
VERA	You must be mad.
SUSAN	Why, I could do it easy. My brother can get me a bunch of master ignition keys.
VERA	Oh for heavens sake, Sue, be your age. For a start, how many nuns have you seen driving a Jag?

SUSAN   Oh yes, I see what you mean.

VERA   You would have the whole world staring at you.

BESS   Hold on. She doesn't have to wear a habit does she? She
             could do it in civvies.

VERA   (thinking a moment)   That's a point. Do you reckon
             you could?

SUSAN   Sure.

VERA   We'll keep it in mind then. I'll discuss it with Solly
             tomorrow.

EDITH   What do you reckon we'd get for it?

VERA   I'm not sure what the market price is at the moment.

BESS   We ought to get a minimum of five hundred anyway. It
             would be a change to be able to dictate terms.

EDITH   I think we ought to plan this very carefully. If Solly
             doesn't play we could get landed with it.

SUSAN   Oh we could flog it easily enough. Jean, your old man
             could shift it couldn't he?

JEAN   Yes - when he comes out.

BESS   How much longer has he got?

JEAN   With good behaviour, seven years.

SUSAN   Oh.

EDITH   I'm not so sure it is a good idea after all. Let's face it,
             we are specialists in our own line and I think we'd be mad
             to branch out into another field where we haven't the
             knowhow or the outlets. One slip up could smash the
             whole business.

JEAN   How?

EDITH   Supposing Susan was copped with the car before she got
             the chance to deliver it?

SUSAN   (annoyed)   Do you think I'd grass on you?

EDITH   I'm sure you wouldn't, but supposing the press got hold of
             the story, after all it is something unusual, a woman car

snatcher.

JEAN   I don't see what you are getting at.

EDITH   Simply this. If her photo appeared in the National Press,
              it's possible that someone, and maybe someone who has
              had stuff nicked off them, might look at it and say, 'I know
              that woman, I've seen her before, only the last time she
              was a nun'. It wouldn't take the narks very long to put
              two and two together and they would be round here like a
              dose of salts.

VERA   That's positive thinking Edith. Thanks. In view of that I
              think we'd better scrub the idea.

SUSAN   (irritably)   Why don't you keep your big trap shut? I
              would have loved to have done that job.

EDITH   (grimly)   Because I don't want another spell in the
              nick, that's why.

SUSAN   (angrily)   The trouble with an old bag of wind like you
              is -

VERA   (bangs table)   All right, all right, that's enough. The
              deal is off and that's final.

SUSAN   (sourly)   It's five hundred nicker down the drain and
              whichever way you look at it, that's a ton apiece.
              (Sighs.)   Oh well, if you say so.

              (There is a pause.)

BESS   Are we going to do the housekeeping job this afternoon?

VERA   No, it's a bit late. We'll buy the stuff this weekend.

BESS   Well if that's the case I'll get into some comfortable gear.
              (She wanders out right.)

              (There is a pause. The others take off their veils, except
              VERA who is examining the lists again. Everyone is
              smoking. JEAN wanders to the window.)

JEAN   Vera?

VERA   Mmn?

JEAN   When are we moving?

VERA	Moving what?
JEAN	Getting out of this place.
VERA	Oh that, I hadn't fixed a date. Why?
JEAN	I was talking to Edith just now about the garden.
VERA	(still absorbed) What about it?
JEAN	I'd like to take it in hand and grow flowers and vegetables.
VERA	(looking up) You must be joking.
JEAN	No, I'm serious.
VERA	Well, what do you know? We have a market gardener in our midst.
JEAN	Oh turn it up. Just because I'm a hoist by profession, it doesn't mean to say I haven't got a hobby.
VERA	No I suppose not. I should forget about it though. We won't be here long enough.
JEAN	But do we have to go?
VERA	We'd be mugs to stay too long. Besides we can't work this area indefinitely, they would be bound to tumble to it sooner or later.
JEAN	We don't have to work this area at all. We could establish our respectability by staying here indefinitely and make a point of buying everything locally.
VERA	Am I being very dense?
SUSAN	I think I see what she is getting at. (To JEAN.) You mean leave this area clear, just use it as our head-quarters and work other areas right outside?
JEAN	Yes. Birmingham, Leicester, Stoke, Liverpool, Nottingham and so on. Work the round. They are all easily accessible by train, we could leave early in the morning and be back by tea.
VERA	(suddenly) You know what, I think you've hit it. Edith, let's have that A.A. book from the mantelpiece.
	(EDITH brings it across to her.)

EDITH   It would do away with all the trouble of finding a new
                  place every three months, which in time is bound to be
                  suspicious.

SUSAN   That's a good point. We could even build up our
                  respectability here by helping with the odd do's like
                  jumble sales, bazaars and collecting for the old folk.

VERA   Watch it mate, before you've finished you'll have us all
                  taking our vows.

SUSAN   (smiles)   I wouldn't go that far but I think it's
                  something we could work on.

VERA   (sits back, thinking)   Yes, the more I think of it the
                  better it sounds. Who is going to associate a hoist in
                  Manchester with a small group of nuns a hundred miles
                  away?

JEAN   Exactly.

VERA   Let's look at the map.

                  (They spread it out and gather round.)

                  Now, let's see the best way to work this.

EDITH   Well, we're roughly in the centre of all these places, let's
                  gradually work round the edge.

VERA   No, that's too obvious, it calls for cut and thrust raids,
                  north one day, south east the next, south west the next and
                  so forth. Then a break of a week so there is no definite
                  pattern. We could either work it as a team or on a rota
                  basis in pairs. Mark you, it's going to be more tiring with
                  all this extra travelling but the risk of detection is brought
                  to a minimum.

EDITH   You don't think the locals will question our always
                  travelling by rail?

VERA   Why should they? Our calling as collectors takes us all
                  over the country.

JEAN   (smiling)   Well there is one thing, we will always be
                  sure of a seat.

                  (They all laugh. The door bell rings. They stop laughing.)

EDITH   What was that?

SUSAN   I think it was the door bell.

             (The bell rings again.)

VERA   You are right. Who the hell can be calling on us here?

             (JEAN runs to the window, glances out.)

JEAN   (aghast)   Oh gawd!

VERA   What?

JEAN   There's a couple of nuns outside.

VERA   They can't be.

JEAN   I'm damn sure they are not penguins. Come and have a
             look.

             (They all hurriedly crowd round the window.)

SUSAN   What the hell do we do?

VERA   Send them away with some excuse, perhaps this is just a
             duty call.

EDITH   Duty call my foot, they've got two trunks and they have
             sent the taxi away.

             (The bell rings again.)

SUSAN   Well do something somebody.

VERA   Okay. Leave this to me.   (She leans out of the
             window and calls sweetly.)   I will be down in a
             moment, we have just finished our –   (She cannot
             think of the word, she glances wildly at the others for
             help.)

SUSAN   (quickly)   Devotions.

VERA   (whispering)   Ta.   (Out of window again.)
             – our devotions.   (She turns to the others, rapping out
             orders.)   Well don't just stand there. Put your veils
             on – empty these ash trays and get rid of this smoke. And
             for pete's sake tidy this place up, it looks like a doss
             house. I'll go and let them in and delay them as much as
             possible. Go on now, go, go, go.

(VERA starts to leave as they begin to tidy the place frantically.)

JEAN   Hey, Vera. Who are we supposed to be?

VERA   (testily)   Nuns you clot, nuns.

JEAN   I know that but what is the order?

VERA   Oh that! – the er – er – Sisters of Benefaction, quite new, founded six months ago.   (She hurries out.)

JEAN   Right, just so we stick to the same story.

SUSAN   Oh lor, this is all I need.

EDITH   (suddenly)   Lipstick!

SUSAN   What about it?

EDITH   Wipe it off!

SUSAN   Oh, of course. Ta.   (She wipes her lips vigorously.)

                (They flap newspapers around frantically, hide things behind cushions, etc. and adjust their veils. After a pause, VERA enters followed by two stately nuns.)

VERA   Will you come this way?

                (They come into the room.)

                Sisters, may I introduce Sister Angela and Sister Rose of the order of Magnus.

                (The two nuns nod kindly.)

                This is Sister Jean, Sister Edith and Sister Susan.

ANGELA   And you are the Mother Superior I presume?

VERA   Er – that is correct. Yes.

                (There is an awkward pause.)

ANGELA   Do you think we might sit down, we are rather tired.

VERA   Of course, of course, what am I thinking of? Make yourselves comfortable.

ANGELA   Thank you.

                (They both sit on settee.)

Oh that's very gratifying. Yes, we have been on the move since five o'clock this morning.

JEAN   Five o'clock! You poor dev-   er people. What about a nice cup of tea?

ANGELA   That's a real Christian thought.

JEAN   Or something stronger perhaps?

ANGELA   (perplexed)   Stronger?

VERA   (quickly)   She means coffee.

ANGELA   Oh. That sounds delightful. Coffee for you, Sister?

ROSE   Thank you.

EDITH   I'll go and make it.   (She goes out.)

ANGELA   I feel we are intruding on your privacy here.

VERA   (airily)   Oh not at all.

ANGELA   You see we have a roving commission as it were. We go out into the world for six months at a time, carrying on the good work you know and sheltering, as you might say, wherever there is a kindly roof.

ROSE   They are hard to find, too.

ANGELA   Oh yes, for us it is a miracle to find a haven like this.

VERA   If I may ask, how did you manage to find us?

ANGELA   We made enquiries in town at one of the shops and the proprietor told us he thought there was a convent out this way as he had noticed you people in town.

VERA   That was very obliging of him.

ANGELA   Yes, actually he seemed quite pleased to see us. It appears that someone had stolen a valuable pair of binoculars from his window and he was most upset. He said, 'The town needs honest people like you instead of the thugs and er, er - '

ROSE   Layabouts.

ANGELA   Oh yes, 'Layabouts, we have to contend with'.

ROSE   So we hired a taxi and after a lot of trouble tracked you down.

ANGELA
It was pure luck really. You haven't a sign on your gate at the end of the drive and the building can't be seen from the road at all.

VERA
No, well you see, we haven't been here very long ourselves. We've only recently taken over this place and haven't had the time to do all that we wanted.

ANGELA
I must say it's very charming and most secluded. Are you here permanently?

JEAN
I hope so.

VERA
(quickly)   Don't interrupt, Sister.

JEAN
(meekly)   I'm sorry, Mother.

VERA
As I was saying, our own plans are rather indefinite at the moment. Ours is quite a new and different order and we have to move around quite a lot. Our finances, of course, are rather limited and we managed to rent this establishment very cheaply as it had been on the market a long time. Whether we can afford to keep it on remains to be seen.

ANGELA
I see, it all sounds rather exciting.

SUSAN
Oh yes, life is quite a trial, isn't it, Mother?

(VERA gives her a fixed smile. The phone rings and she picks it up.)

VERA
Mother Superior speaking, can I help you? - Well, Father, I'd better discuss that with you tomorrow -

(ANGELA goes to the window and glances out.)

ANGELA
What a charming view from here. Come and have a look, Sister.

(Sister ROSE joins her.)

VERA
(firmly)   I can't possibly answer that, Father -
(She cups her hand round the mouthpiece and whispers harshly into it.)   Solly, you stupid git, get off the line -   (Kindly.)   Yes, yes - and blessings upon you, too.   (She puts the phone down firmly.)

I must apologise, the Reverend Father is most persistent.

ANGELA (smiles) That's quite all right, we understand, don't we, Sister?

ROSE Oh yes.

ANGELA We have to deal with those in our order too. I was just saying what a peaceful place this is. I think we shall be very happy here.

VERA Er – how long were you contemplating staying?

ROSE Well as long as –

ANGELA (interrupting) Well, shall we say, two or three –

VERA Days?

ANGELA No. Months.

VERA Months!

ANGELA You don't mind?

VERA Oh – er – of course not.

ANGELA We couldn't accept your charity of course, we are quite willing to contribute towards our keep. We naturally can't afford very much, but I am sure we could spare thirty shillings for each of us per week.

VERA (falsely) Well it all helps, doesn't it?

(BESS suddenly enters wearing a ridiculous hat. She doesn't see the visitors.)

BESS Hey, what do you think of my dolly hat? Dead kinky, isn't it? You can pick up anything at the sales and nobody challenges you when you come out.

VERA (firmly, to SUSAN) Sister, would you take Sister Bess back to her room, I think she had better lie down again.

SUSAN Very well, Mother, come along, Sister.

BESS (protesting) What do you think you are doing? Keep your thieving hands to yourself.

(SUSAN steers her towards the door. She whispers to her urgently.)

SUSAN   (whispering)   We have company, you idiot.

                (BESS stops, turns round and sees the visitors.)

BESS   Oh gawd!   (Realising that she is supposed to be a nun,
                she makes a vague gesture somewhere between a dip of the
                knee and a curtsey, nearly falling over in the effort. As
                she straightens she lets out a loud hiccup.)   Peace be
                with you.

                (SUSAN almost races her out of the room. There is an
                embarrassed silence.)

VERA   (clearing her throat)   I must apologise, I'm afraid we
                have rather a problem. You see, Sister Bess is - well -
                (She taps her forehead.)   not exactly unbalanced -
                shall we be charitable and say, eccentric and rather
                unreliable. We have to watch her the whole time.

ANGELA   I feel very sorry for you. What a dreadful responsibility.

VERA   Oh she's a good worker but as I say, one can't depend on
                her.

                (EDITH enters with two cups of coffee.)

EDITH   Your coffee, Sisters.

ANGELA   Oh how kind.

VERA   I tell you what, as you are staying why not have it in
                your room and you can freshen up as well. We'll take
                your trunks up for you later.

ANGELA   Thank you, Mother, that is most kind.

VERA   Take them up, Sister Edith, the big room in the east wing,
                then come back here as I have other duties for you.

ANGELA   We will be down shortly.

EDITH   Will you follow me?   (She leads the way out carrying
                the tray.)

                (The visitors trail after her. There is a long silence.)

VERA   (quietly)   I don't believe it. It isn't really happening
                to us, is it?

JEAN   I'm afraid so. I must say you handled it marvellously.

VERA   Maybe, but how long can we keep it up?

JEAN   Not for three months, that's for sure.

VERA   Oh lor, I'd forgotten that. Get the other two down here
                as quickly as possible.

JEAN   Right.   (She hurries out.)

                (VERA goes to the phone and dials. After a moment she
                speaks.)

VERA   Solly? Vera here - now listen very carefully. Whatever
                you do, don't ring here again, I'll explain everything
                when I see you tomorrow - oh shut up about your flaming
                Jag, we are not doing that job after all -   Look we've
                got troubles too mate - oh, get lost.   (She slams the
                phone down.)

                (JEAN, SUSAN and BESS enter.)

BESS   (angrily)   Why the hell didn't you warn me?

VERA   (angrily)   Why didn't you look, you stupid cow?

BESS   (shouting)   Well how was I to know?

SUSAN   (urgently)   For heaven's sake keep your voice down.

BESS   (whispering)   Nobody told me you had company.

VERA   (whispering)   We didn't know ourselves.   (In a
                normal voice.)   Oh, what the hell am I whispering
                for?

                (EDITH enters.)

                Well?

EDITH   They are washing.

VERA   That gives us about ten minutes.

EDITH   I wouldn't bank on it. They told me they would bring
                their coffee down here. You weren't very clever, were
                you?

VERA   What do you mean?

EDITH   We've got all last week's loot stashed away in the room
                next to theirs.

VERA   Oh blimey, I'd forgotten.

EDITH   Don't worry, I locked the door, here is the key.

VERA   Phew! Good for you.

JEAN   What's the plan Vera?

VERA   Well, first and foremost they mustn't rumble us.

EDITH   Oh we can hold our own for a couple of days.

JEAN   A couple of days, my aunt fanny. They are stopping three months.

EDITH   What!

VERA   That's their idea but we've got to find some way of getting rid of them.

EDITH   I should cocoa, we couldn't afford to keep them.

VERA   (stonily)   They are paying thirty bob towards their keep.

JEAN   I should think the big one would eat at least a tenners worth on her own.

VERA   That's beside the point, right now we've got to cover up and that means no smoking for a start.

           (They all groan and murmur.)

           And you Bess have got to lay off the liquor - phew I can smell the gin from here. Someone give her some peppermints.

BESS   I hate peppermints.

VERA   (grimly)   You'll learn to love them. Cram them into her mouth if necessary.

           (JEAN takes a bag of peppermints from her pocket and advances on BESS.)

BESS   (defiantly)   All right then, if you don't mind my throwing up.

VERA   (grimly)   We'll take the risk.

           (JEAN forces BESS to take a mouthful.)

SUSAN	What next?
VERA	Our rooms. Get every piece of clothing out of sight (To SUSAN.) especially those fancy pants of yours. All liquor bottles stored away, make the beds and don't forget to hide your cigarettes.
JEAN	I can't give up fags just like that.
VERA	You'll have to – we'll all have to, while they are in the house.
JEAN	Well all I can say is that I'll have to have a crafty drag in the loo like we used to at school.
VERA	That's up to you but watch it. Right come on everybody, clear the decks and heaven help anyone who leaves anything around that could give us away.
BESS	I think I'll stay here.
VERA	Oh no you won't, you are our greatest handicap.
BESS	I feel as sick as a dog.
VERA	(tersely) Well you know where the bathroom is. Come on.
	(JEAN and SUSAN bustle a protesting BESS out and EDITH and VERA follow. As they reach the door, the two visitors enter the other door. VERA turns.)
	Oh, finished already?
ANGELA	Yes, we just freshened up. We thought we'd have our coffee down here. Are we disturbing you?
VERA	Oh not at all.
EDITH	We are all going to sort out some clothes for a jumble sale.
ANGELA	Oh how splendid. We'll help you.
VERA	Oh I wouldn't dream of accepting, especially after your long journey. Sit down and have a rest, we won't be very long.
ANGELA	Well if you insist.
VERA	I do. Come along, Sister. (She goes out followed by EDITH.)

(ANGELA sits on the settee and sips her coffee. ROSE
crosses to the right door and glances out.)

ANGELA   (smiling)   Well, Sister Rose?

ROSE   Don't give me that Sister lark any more, Angy. As it is
              you never let me get a word in from the moment we arrived.
              I tell you, I felt a right burke sitting there.

ANGELA   Well I know you and your language, I didn't want to take
              the risk.

ROSE   Why come here in the first place?

ANGELA   I keep telling you, because it's the perfect cover. Where
              else do you expect to find nuns but in a convent?

ROSE   But they are bound to find out.

ANGELA   Not if you keep your trap shut. Don't forget they are
              simple people, they only see good in others.

ROSE   Well all I can say is they must have flipping good eyesight
              to see anything good in us.

ANGELA   All we have to do is to be careful.

ROSE   Another thing, how are we going to store the stuff we nick?

ANGELA   There are two huge cupboards in our room, I've got the key
              and we'll keep them locked. In any case who is going to
              search?

ROSE   I tell you I don't like it. We'd be better off getting a pad
              of our own.   (She takes out a packet of cigarettes.)

ANGELA   Hey, watch your step.

ROSE   It's all right for you, you are a non smoker but if I don't
              have a drag I'll bust.   (She lights up.)

ANGELA   Put it out you fool, they will be back in a minute.

ROSE   Not on your nelly, they will be hours over that lot. I've
              done jumble sales before, I know. All right then, you
              keep watch by the door and I'll smoke up the chimney if it
              makes you feel any happier.

ANGELA   (sighs)   All right.   (She moves to the door and
              stands guard.)

(ROSE goes to the fire and gets on her knees blowing the smoke up the chimney.)

ROSE   (contentedly)   Oh God bless you, Sir Walter Raleigh.

(There is a pause.)

ANGELA   I've been thinking.

ROSE   If it's anything to improve my image you can forget it.

ANGELA   No. I know now how to get the stuff out of here.

ROSE   I'll buy it.

ANGELA   They've got a sort of broken down old Black Maria in the garage.

ROSE   Oh gawd, don't mention that word.

ANGELA   I noticed it as the taxi drew up, they must use that as their transport.

ROSE   They are welcome.

ANGELA   We could ask them if we can borrow it one day a week, I'm sure they wouldn't mind if we fill the tank up for them each time.

ROSE   You mean, use it for jobs?

ANGELA   No to get the stuff out at the end of the week and run it down to the fence.

ROSE   You must be joking.

ANGELA   No, it's dead easy.

ROSE   All right, brains, convince me.

ANGELA   We pack the stuff into brown paper parcels and if they want to know where we are taking them, it's to distribute among the needy people.

ROSE   That's not bad. Hey wait a mo, supposing they want to help?

ANGELA   Oh they can't do that, it's a very strict rule of our order that we are not allowed to work with members of another order.

ROSE   (admiringly)   I've got to hand it to you Angy, I'd never have thought of that.

ANGELA   (drily)   No, I know.

ROSE   I wonder if there is anything worth nicking here. Don't they have silver plate and stuff?

ANGELA   (quickly)   Don't be a mug, that would be the first thing to give us away.

ROSE   I suppose there wouldn't be anything worth taking anyway. Hey talking of that, you know that shop where we asked that geezer for this address?

ANGELA   Yes.

ROSE   We might try that place. He's got two German cameras on a shelf near the door simply asking to be whipped.

ANGELA   You never learn do you, Rosie. That place will be hot for weeks to come. No, we'll spread out.   (Irritably.) Oh for crying out loud, haven't you finished that fag yet?

ROSE   Okay, I'll finish it later.   (She pinches out the end and puts the butt back in the packet then waves the smoke away.)

ANGELA   (going to the settee)   Now as I see it, we can work all the big towns in a wide circle. It will mean having to travel by train but it will be a lot safer. We can use this as our headquarters.

ROSE   It would be easier to work this district.

ANGELA   Maybe but it's safer not to. I think it would be a good idea to establish ourselves as being authentic here.

ROSE   Or what?

ANGELA   Authentic.

ROSE   What are you talking about?

ANGELA   Well to put it in simple language, make people think we are the real thing. I suggest we join these people here, help them occasionally with their work – for a start we could give them a hand with their jumble sale.

ROSE   (firmly)   Oh no.

ANGELA   It would be a good cover.

ROSE   Maybe, but have you ever done one?

ANGELA   Not personally.

ROSE   Then you don't know what you are letting yourself in for. In my youth I used to belong to a drama society and we had them every three months to pay for the shows we lost money on. I tell you, they are killers.

ANGELA   We don't have to do more than a token gesture, something now and then, just to establish ourselves.

ROSE   Okay then, just as long as you don't let this 'do good' bug get a hold on you.

ANGELA   That's settled then.

ROSE   (sighing)   I suppose so.

                (VERA enters followed by the others.)

ANGELA   Finished?

VERA   Yes, thank you.

ANGELA   When is the sale?

VERA   Er - in about three days time.

ANGELA   Sister Rose and I would like to help you.

SUSAN   (quickly)   Oh that's all right, Sister, we can cope. We always do.

ANGELA   Nonsense, we insist. I feel it is the least we can do.

VERA   Well, we'll see nearer the time, shall we?

ANGELA   Yes. We would be a great asset, I know. Sister Rose is an expert on the subject. She's just been telling me.

                (There is an awkward pause.)

JEAN   I'm afraid you won't be very comfortable in your rooms, they are very damp. That's why we don't use that part of the house.

ANGELA   Oh that won't affect us. We are very hardy, aren't we, Sister?

(ROSE doesn't answer, she gets a nudge from ANGELA.)

ROSE (suddenly) Oh yes, very hardy.

SUSAN I'm afraid we live very simply here – well, food is so expensive you see.

JEAN Yes, we were only discussing before you arrived the possibility of growing vegetables in the garden in time, but at the moment, of course, we barely exist. I'm sure you would be more comfortable elsewhere.

ROSE (rising) Yes, I think you are right.

(ANGELA drags her down quickly.)

ANGELA Not at all. Spartan living helps to strengthen one's faith. If it's biscuits and water for you, then it's biscuits and water for us.

VERA (sighing) Very well then, if that is your wish.

ANGELA (sweetly) Oh it is. (Sighs.) I can't tell you what a wonderful feeling it is to have landed in real Christian surroundings.

(BESS hiccups loudly.)

BESS (muttering) Manners.

EDITH (quickly) It's the peppermints.

ROSE Peppermints?

EDITH She suffers from indigestion, peppermints always give her hiccups.

ANGELA Oh my dear, I am sorry.

VERA (sweetly) Don't worry, she'll get over it. We'll see to that.

(There is an awkward pause again.)

ANGELA Well Mother, I suppose about now you have prayers.

VERA Prayers? – oh yes, prayers.

ANGELA Splendid, we always have them about this time and we'd like to join in if we may.

VERA Of course.

(VERA looks at the others who shrug their shoulders. They are out of their depth in the situation.

Oh dear, with all the tidying up I seem to have mislaid my book.

ANGELA   That's no trouble, use mine.

(She produces one from her pocket and hands it to the startled VERA who looks at the others for support but gets none. VERA opens the book wildly and raises her eyes to the ceiling in resignation.)

VERA   (resignedly)   Shall we all kneel?

(Dutifully and with difficulty they all kneel. VERA finds some prayers in the book, clears her throat and prepares to start. There is a loud hiccup from BESS. VERA shuts her eyes as if to shut out the nightmare as the lights fade quickly to a black out.

BLACK OUT

Scene 2   The same, two weeks later

VERA is standing by the window looking out. EDITH is sitting on the settee. SUSAN stands with her back to the fire and JEAN is sitting on the long table. There is a pause.

SUSAN   Well, Vera?

VERA   (irritably)   Well what?

SUSAN   What are we going to do? We can't go on like this, it's hopeless. We haven't done a job for two weeks now.

EDITH   You and your idea of establishing ourselves!

VERA   We had decided to do that in the first place.

JEAN   Yes but not something nearly every day. Every W.I. and Townswomen's Guild for miles around has latched on to us free slave labour. I can see them in their committee meetings, the chairman says, 'Who can we get to help?'

and some old tart staggers up and says, 'I propose we ask the nuns' - and it is carried unanimously in a flash.

(The phone rings. JEAN picks it up.)

Hullo, Stonegate Convent -   The Mother Superior?

(VERA gestures 'No' vehemently.)

I'm sorry but she has just retired to bed, the fête this afternoon was a little too much for her - No, I'm sorry, I can't give you a decision on that - very well, I'll tell her you rang.   (She replaces the receiver.)   Another bazaar next week.

EDITH	If I ever get another cake stall, I'll emigrate.
SUSAN	Yes and they had to give Bess the bottle stall of all things.
JEAN	Talking of that have you noticed something about her?
VERA	What do you mean?
JEAN	She's changed, she's gone all holy or something.
VERA	Yes, now that you mention it, she has been different lately.
JEAN	This 'do good' lark has gone to her head. She loves these do's. Last night I caught her canvassing for more.
EDITH	No!
JEAN	Honest.
SUSAN	I always thought she was bent, that clinches it.
	(BESS enters, gaily.)
BESS	Clinches what?
SUSAN	You, gone all pure.
BESS	I can't help it. I've sort of seen the light. It's done something to me. I get a real kick out of helping these people. Do you know, it may sound awful but right now I feel I couldn't nick another thing to save my life?
EDITH	You are off the bottle too, aren't you?
BESS	Yes, haven't had a drop for over a week now.

SUSAN   (firmly)   That settles it, Vera, you've got to do
something and quick.

VERA   You are right. So'ly rang me yesterday. He is doing his
nut. Wants to know what the hell is going on. He's way
behind with his orders and says that if we don't produce
something pretty quick we'll have to find another fence.

JEAN   Apart from which we haven't earned a penny for two weeks
now.

SUSAN   If only you'd let me knock that Jag off we'd have enough
to tide us over.

VERA   No, definitely not. Somehow we have got to get rid of
these two old bags.

EDITH   That's what we keep saying, but how? Apart from anything
else I just couldn't take another week of bread and soup
with sardines as a treat.

VERA   (firmly)   I agree. We've just got to find a way right
now.   (Looks out of window.)   Oh gawd, here
they come now. Come on,we'll all go to my room.

ALL   Okay.

(They put out their cigarettes and flap papers to disperse
the smoke. The panic in this has gone, it is now purely
routine. They troop out through one door. After a pause
ANGELA and ROSE enter through the other. ANGELA
crosses to the other door, goes out and comes in again.)

ANGELA   (tersely)   Okay, they are in their rooms.

ROSE   Thank heaven for that.   (She flops in the settee and
lights a cigarette.)

ANGELA   (testily)   I wish you'd watch your smoking, I could
still smell the smoke as I came in just now and the place
has been empty all day.

ROSE   Hard luck. I'm not going without me fags as well.

ANGELA   As well as what?

ROSE   Me grub for a start and all this flippin' missionary work
we've been stuck with these last two weeks. Do you know
what I got landed with this afternoon? I'll tell you.

Raffling a pig. My mouth was almost slobbering. I could see it all brown and crackly on a dish with an onion in its mouth, beans, roast spuds and apple sauce.   (She snaps out of her dream.)   I tell you, I've had it and my feet are killing me.

ANGELA   Well I must admit I didn't think we'd have so much to do.

ROSE   One thing is certain, we'll have to start work soon or we'll be skint.

ANGELA   That's true. I've been thinking,Rosie. I was wondering if we couldn't get rid of them somehow.

ROSE   Don't be stupid, this is their place.

ANGELA   I know that but if we could find something – some reason for them to leave, we could stay on here.

ROSE   What for instance?

ANGELA   I don't know. I've toyed with the idea of saying the place was haunted.

ROSE   Ah come off it, that wouldn't work. They would get over that by exercising it or something.

ANGELA   (sighing)   Exorcise.

ROSE   Well, you know what I mean.

ANGELA   There must be something.

ROSE   Well whatever it is you'd better think of it soon because I can't keep this up much longer. My knees will never be the same after all these prayers. Oh gawd, what I wouldn't do for a pint of wallop right now.

(The phone rings. ANGELA answers it.)

ANGELA   Hullo? – No, she's upstairs. This is Sister Angela – Hey wait a minute, is that you Solly? – Well how the hell did you know we were here? How did you get the number? – You didn't know we were here – you what? You do business with Vera! – the same line as us? Oh no, and we thought – never mind, I'll ring you back later. (She puts the phone down and collapses into uncontrollable laughter.)

ROSE

Angy, what's the matter? Pull yourself together, what's happened?

ANGELA

(still laughing)   That was Solly.

ROSE

Well what's so funny in that?

ANGELA

He – he wasn't ringing us, he was ringing them.

ROSE

Them?

ANGELA

Yes, this lot, the Sisters of Benefaction.

(It slowly dawns on ROSE.)

ROSE

You don't mean?

ANGELA

Yes, they are as bent as a corkscrew. They are not nuns, they are in the same racket and using the same cover as us.

ROSE

(angrily)   Well the flaming hypocrites.

ANGELA

And we've all been killing ourselves with all this charity work this last fortnight to impress each other.   (She dissolves into laughter again.)

ROSE

I don't see what is so funny.

ANGELA

(pulling herself together)   No I suppose not really, but don't you see, Rosie old girl, we've got 'em cold.

ROSE

Have we? How?

ANGELA

Don't you see? We know they are crooks but they still think we are the genuine article.

ROSE

Of course.

ANGELA

Now let me think for a minute – I've got it.

ROSE

What?

ANGELA

Well don't you see, we've got them over a barrel, we've got a nap hand, we can put the black on them till it hurts.

ROSE

I still don't get it.

ANGELA

(irritably)   Oh you are so thick I often wonder what keeps your ears apart.

ROSE

(angrily)   Well if it comes to that you are no oil painting yourself.

ANGELA   Oh skip it. Rosie, we are made, we are set up. Get them
                down here and we'll all have a nice cosy little chat.

ROSE   Well tell me, what are we going to chat them up about?

ANGELA   Just leave that to me. Call them down.

ROSE   (grumbling)   I just hope you know what you are at.

ANGELA   I do.

                (ROSE crosses to door.)

                Put your fag out you clot.

ROSE   Oh – oh yes.   (She stubs it out on her shoe and puts
                the butt in her pocket then goes out.)

                (ANGELA rubs her hands together in anticipation and goes
                to the window. After a pause they all troop in.)

VERA   (sweetly)   You wanted to see us?

ANGELA   (sweetly)   Yes, it is the question of leaving this
                place.

                (They all glance at each other hardly able to conceal their
                smiles of relief.)

                Shall we sit down?

VERA   Of course. Sisters, make yourselves comfortable.

                (They all sit then ANGELA comes down to the table.)

ANGELA   Now what I am going to say may come as a shock but I feel
                I must say it.

VERA   Of course, of course.

ANGELA   We have been very comfortable here, very comfortable
                indeed.

VERA   I am so pleased to hear that. We only did our humble
                best.

ANGELA   In fact we have all worked together admirably.

VERA   It's been a very pleasant experience altogether.

ANGELA   I had hoped it could continue indefinitely, but all good
                things come to an end.

VERA	We are only sorry to see you go.
ANGELA	I think you misunderstand me. We are not going.
SUSAN	No?
ANGELA	(sweetly) No, we suggest that you leave.
JEAN	What are you talking about?
ANGELA	It has come to our notice, quite by accident I assure you, that you ladies are not what you appear to be.
VERA	(standing) I beg your pardon.
ANGELA	It would appear that you are not nuns at all but common thieves, a gang of shop lifters.
	(There is a dreadful silence.)
VERA	(grimly) You have proof of this?
ANGELA	Oh yes, undisputable proof.
ROSE	Aren't you ashamed of yourselves?
ANGELA	Be quiet, Sister.
VERA	What are you going to do about it?
ANGELA	(to window) It is a very difficult decision for me. My first impulse naturally was to inform the authorities and then I remembered how valiantly you had all worked at these various charities during the last two weeks and I realised that deep down there must be a lot of good in you, and I just couldn't bring myself to being responsible for having you committed to prison.
SUSAN	You mean you won't grass on us?
ANGELA	Grass?
SUSAN	(sighing) Tell the police.
ANGELA	No.
EDITH	That's very decent of you.
ANGELA	I searched my heart to find some way in which I could salve my own conscience and you in your turn could atone to a certain degree for your sins.

VERA	And what did you decide?
ANGELA	Briefly that you return the money you have gained from your nefarious exploits.
VERA	But how could we do that?
ANGELA	Oh I don't mean to the people you have robbed. I mean in a different form, to people who need it more.
VERA	I don't follow you.
ANGELA	It is quite simple really. Our order is very poor, perhaps a substantial donation –
ROSE	In cash.
ANGELA	Naturally, Sister – this would enable us to carry on our good work and as you will not be requiring this house in the circumstances, perhaps you would make that over to us for our headquarters.
VERA	(angrily) That's blackmail.
ANGELA	That's a very ugly word. Shall we say – atonement?
	(VERA thinks for a moment, she is furious.)
VERA	We won't do it!
ROSE	Do you want the police to know?
SUSAN	Of course not.
VERA	Look, we've got to have time to discuss this among ourselves.
ANGELA	There really isn't anything to discuss.
	(BESS starts to giggle, it gets uncontrollable. She flops on the settee.)
SUSAN	Oh hell, she's been at the bottle again.
JEAN	At a time like this, too.
EDITH	(testily) Oh shut up, Bess.
BESS	I can't help it, it is so funny.
ANGELA	(coldly) What is so funny?
BESS	The self righteous look on your face.

ANGELA   I beg your pardon.

BESS   And to think you had the ruddy cheek to blackmail us.

VERA   (quickly)   What are you talking about?

BESS   Didn't you know, they are in the same racket.

ALL   What!

BESS   They are common hoists like us.

ANGELA   The woman is mad.

SUSAN   How do you know?

BESS   Old chubby chops   (Indicating ROSE.)   gave the
game away. Have you ever seen a nun with a pound of
nicotine on her fingers before?

          (ROSE glances at her fingers then hides her hand behind
          her back quickly.)

ANGELA   (angrily)   You stupid clot, I've been on to you about
this all the time.

BESS   So I thought I'd pay their room a little visit and have a
look in their cupboards.

ANGELA   You couldn't, they were locked.

BESS   I picked them with a hair pin.

ROSE   (angrily)   That's criminal.

BESS   Blimey, look who's talking. You should have a look
inside, they are stashed with loot from top to bottom. I
even nicked a camera for myself.

          (There is a silence then ROSE gets furious.)

ROSE   You raving nit, Angy. This is all your fault. I told you
to flog the stuff right away and now look what's happened.

VERA   When did you find out about this, Bess?

BESS   The second day they were here.

SUSAN   Why didn't you tell us before?

BESS   Because I was enjoying myself at all these do's. It's the
first chance I've ever had of being respectable and I

           thought I'd carry on a little longer just for a giggle.

ROSE   Oh well, that's torn it, good and proper.

           (There is a pause while they sum up the situation.)

EDITH   Well it looks like stalemate, doesn't it?

ANGELA   (sullenly)   I suppose so.

           (Everyone takes off their veils, light cigarettes, etc.)

VERA   One thing I don't understand. How did you rumble us?

ROSE   Solly rang just now.

VERA   Well even so, he wouldn't let on.

ROSE   He didn't. Angy recognised his voice.

           (They look puzzled.)

           Don't you see? Solly fences for us too.

VERA   Oh no.

           (They all see the funny side of it and laugh.)

           Tell me, Angy, where did you learn to talk so posh?

ANGELA   I used to be a school teacher. Why?

VERA   Well with you as our mouthpiece we can't lose.

ANGELA   You mean -

VERA   That we join forces.

ANGELA   Honest?

VERA   Sure. We've got the perfect set up here and can do with
           two extra hands. It will cut the work. We both use the
           same fence and those who aren't out on a job can keep up
           the respectability front by doing social work in the district.
           What do you say, girls?

ALL   Okay. Fair enough, etc.

VERA   Is it a deal?

ANGELA   Done.

           (They shake hands.)

ROSE   Let's celebrate, let's all get stoned.

BESS   I'll get the gin.

ROSE   Any beer?

BESS   Enough to see you off.

ROSE   Good for you, Sister. I'll come and give you a hand.

            (As they start to go out, the doorbell rings.)

VERA   Who on earth?

            (JEAN hurries to the window and looks out.)

JEAN   Oh no!

VERA   What?

JEAN   You'll never believe this but there are a couple of nuns
            outside with trunks.

            (They all look at one another. There is a mad scramble to
            put veils on, extinguish cigarettes and waft smoke as the
            curtain falls.)

            CURTAIN

www.ingramcontent.com/pod-product-compliance
Ingram Content Group UK Ltd.
Pitfield, Milton Keynes, MK11 3LW, UK
UKHW020038170726
7214IPUK00036B/257